GUIDE TO
SPAIN

D0607777

BRIAN WILLIAMS

Highlights for Children

CONTENTS

On the cover: The Plaza de España in Seville, Spain, is brick, covered with bright ceramic tiles. It was built in 1929 for a Spanish-American fair.

Published by Highlights for Children
© 1995 Highlights for Children, Inc.
P.O. Box 18201
Columbus, Ohio 43218-0201
For information on *Top Secret Adventures*, visit
www.tsadventures.com or call 1-800-962-3661.

All rights reserved. No part of this book may be reproduced or transmitted in any form or by any means, electronic or mechanical, including photocopying, recording, or by any information storage and retrieval system, without permission in writing from the publisher.

10 9 8 7 6 5
ISBN 0-87534-921-8

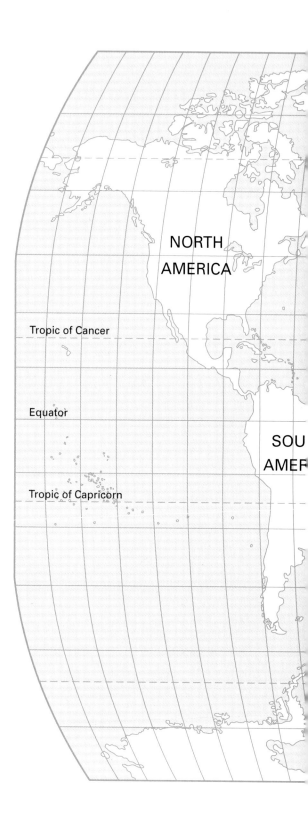

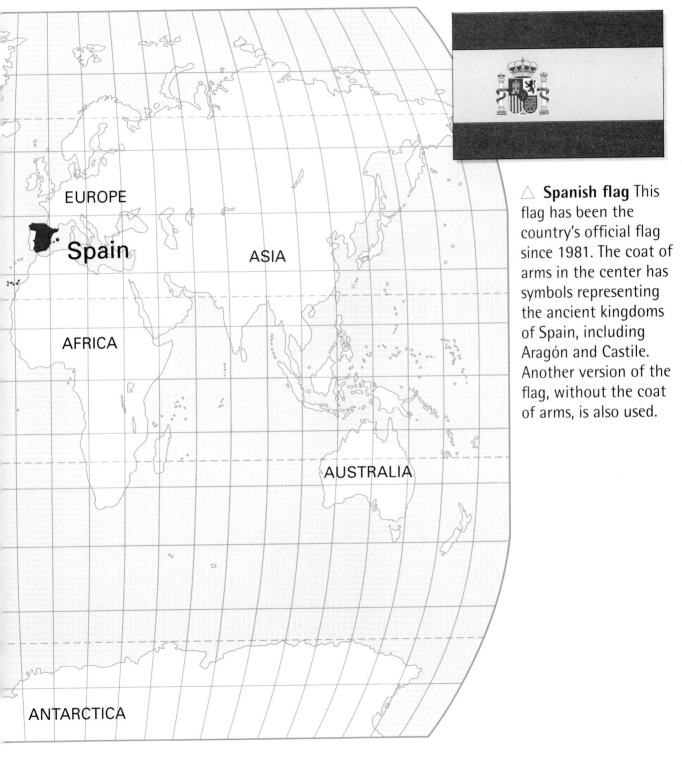

EUROPE

Spain

ASIA

AFRICA

AUSTRALIA

ANTARCTICA

△ **Spanish flag** This flag has been the country's official flag since 1981. The coat of arms in the center has symbols representing the ancient kingdoms of Spain, including Aragón and Castile. Another version of the flag, without the coat of arms, is also used.

3

SPAIN AT A GLANCE

Area 194,855 square miles
(504,782 square kilometers)

Population 39,568,000

Capital Madrid, population of
city and surroundings
3,124,000

Other big city Barcelona
(population 1,694,000)

**Highest mountain on the
mainland** Mulhacén, 11,411
feet (3,478 meters)

Longest river Ebro, 565 miles
(927 kilometers)

Largest lake There are no large
natural lakes in Spain.

Official language Spanish

▽ **Spanish stamps** Two show King Juan Carlos I. The other stamps show police, transportation, science, and the Western European Union.

△ **Spanish money** Spain's currency is the peseta. A new European currency, the euro, was established in January 1999. It is slated to become the sole currency of the European Union countries on July 1, 2002.

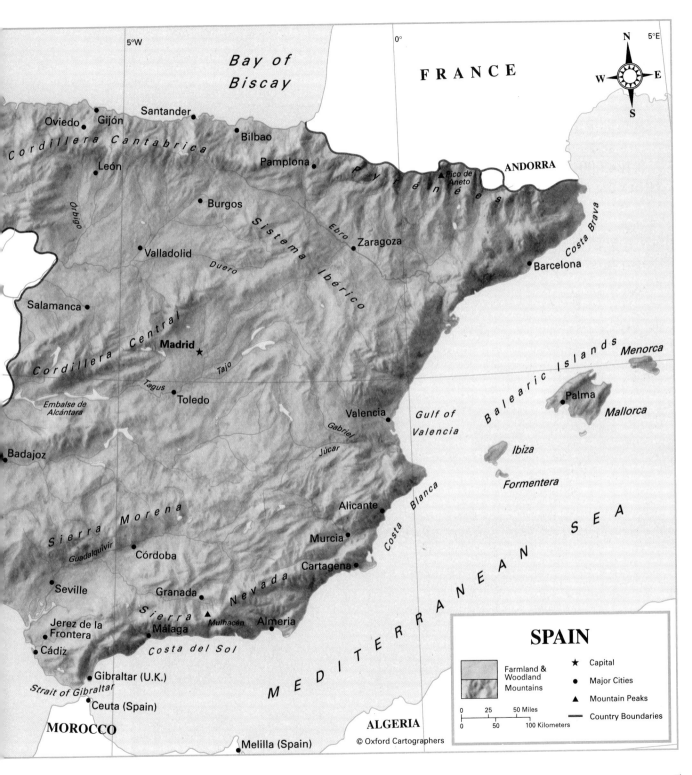

Bay of Biscay

FRANCE

N
W E
S
5°E

5°W

0°

Oviedo • • Gijón Santander •
• Bilbao
Cordillera Cantabrica
León •
Pamplona •
Pyrenées
Pico de Aneto ▲
ANDORRA

Burgos •
Órbigo
Ebro
Sistema Ibérico
Costa Brava

Valladolid •
Duero
Zaragoza •
Barcelona •

Salamanca •

Cordillera Central
Madrid ★

Balearic Islands
Menorca

Tajo
Palma •
Mallorca

Embalse de Alcántara
Tagus
Toledo •

Badajoz •
Valencia •
Gabriel
Gulf of Valencia

Júcar
Ibiza

Formentera

Sierra Morena
Costa Blanca
Alicante •

Guadalquivir
Córdoba •
Murcia •

Cartagena •

Seville •
Nevada
MEDITERRANEAN SEA

Granada •
Sierra
▲ Mulhacén
Almeria •

Jerez de la Frontera •
Málaga •
Costa del Sol

Cádiz •

Gibraltar (U.K.) •

Strait of Gibraltar

Ceuta (Spain) •

MOROCCO

ALGERIA

© Oxford Cartographers

Melilla (Spain) •

SPAIN

Farmland & Woodland
Mountains

★ Capital
• Major Cities
▲ Mountain Peaks
— Country Boundaries

0   25   50 Miles
0   50   100 Kilometers

5

WELCOME TO SPAIN

Spain is a large country in southwestern Europe. From the map you can see why the sea is important to Spain. The country is located on the Iberian Peninsula. To the north and west is the Atlantic Ocean. To the south and east is the Mediterranean Sea. Two groups of islands, the Balearics and the Canary Islands, are part of Spain.

▽ **A festival crowd** Spanish people enjoy festivals and celebrations, which often take place on religious holidays.

Along Spain's northern border with France rise the high Pyrenees Mountains and the smaller Cantabrian Cordillera. To the west, Spain borders the country of Portugal. In the center of Spain is the Meseta, a large flat dry region. *Meseta* is Spanish for "tableland." Few people live here. Mountain ranges, called *sierras* in Spanish, cut across the Meseta. In the south are the Sierra Nevada mountains. This is where you will find Mulhacén, the highest peak on the Spanish mainland.

Major rivers of Spain include the Ebro, Guadalquivir, Duero, and Tajo, or Tagus, Rivers. The Tajo is longer than the Ebro, but it flows westward into Portugal on its way to the sea. Much of Spain's land is dry and hot in summer and cold in winter. Most Spanish people live in cities and in areas where irrigation helps farmers to grow crops, such as the plains along the southeast coast.

Spain became a united country in the 1500s, at the end of the time known as the Middle Ages. Different regions still have their own history, traditions, and languages. The two most independent groups of people are the Basques of the north central region and the Catalans of the northeast.

Spain is a modern nation with a proud and noble past. It is a colorful land of castles and bullfights, cathedrals and sunny tourist beaches, quiet villages and busy industrial cities. Welcome to Spain.

◁ **The Cathedral of the Sagrada Familia (Holy Family) in Barcelona** This unusual and beautiful building was designed by the architect Antonio Gaudí.

▽ **A view of the Costa Blanca** Spain has a long coastline with many fine sandy beaches. Here, in the southeast of Spain, mountains are close to the sea.

HISTORIC MADRID

Madrid, the capital of Spain, is in the center of the country. At 2,150 feet (655 meters) above sea level, it is the highest capital city in Europe. Before the 1500s there were only farmers living here. Then King Philip II made Madrid his capital in 1561. In the 1800s wealthy people from all over Europe came to the city to enjoy its pure air. Today traffic and pollution have made the city air less healthy.

Madrid is a city of many monuments, museums, and royal palaces. It is here that Spain's government meets. The people who live in Madrid are known as *Madrileños*. They enjoy strolling along the city's elegant boulevards. In the heat of summer, morning and evening are the best times for people to meet and do business. In the middle of the day, many people take a break to eat lunch and perhaps to have a short *siesta*, or nap.

▽ **The Plaza España in Madrid** One of the statues in this city square is of Miguel de Cervantes, author of *Don Quixote*.

▷ **Boaters in El Parque del Retiro, Madrid** This public park, with its lovely flowers, statues, and fountains, dates from the 1600s.

A popular meeting place is Puerta del Sol (Gate of the Sun), where there is a statue of a bear with a strawberry tree, the symbol of Madrid. From here visitors can ride buses or subways around the city. They can walk along the Calle Alcalá, one of the city's main avenues. Then, after shopping in the stores on Calle Preciados, it is pleasant to rest among the fountains of El Parque del Retiro, or enjoy the shade of the Botanical Gardens.

The magnificent Royal Palace, built in the 1700s, is one of the older buildings in Madrid. Many of the city's buildings were damaged or destroyed during the Spanish Civil War of 1936-1939. Since then Madrid has grown quickly. In the business area downtown, tall office buildings tower above the streets. New suburbs have sprung up around the city, with homes in some and factories in others.

▽ **Traffic in a busy Madrid street** The capital city is the financial and political center of Spain.

MEET THE PEOPLE

The people of Madrid enjoy visiting the city's many sidewalk cafés. Here they drink coffee or hot chocolate (eaten with a fried dough stick called a *churro*). They may also eat the tasty snacks known as *tapas*. Often people go from one bar or café to the next. They love to try the different tapas each place offers. Most people eat dinner late in the evening and stay up into the night.

Children, and many adults, wear their best clothes to go to church. Older women, especially widows, may still wear all-black clothing. Spain is a religious country. Almost all Spaniards are Roman Catholics.

Many people in Spain enjoy sports. The main soccer stadium in Madrid holds 100,000 people. Huge crowds also go to the bullfights on Sunday afternoons. Madrid's patron saint, St. Isidro, is honored with a bullfighting festival early every summer. It lasts for twenty-seven days, the longest of the many bullfight festivals in Spain.

Art lovers come to Madrid to visit the Prado Museum, one of the world's greatest art galleries. Thousands of world-famous paintings are displayed here, including works by Spanish masters such as Goya and Velázquez. Displayed in the new Centro de Arte Reina Sofía, a modern art museum, is Picasso's famous war painting *Guernica*.

Madrid has many fine shops where you can buy antiques, leatherwork, high-quality clothes and shoes, and guitars. There are also shops selling candy scented with violets. Plaza Mayor, or Main Square, was built in the late 1600s. Cars are not allowed into it. Nearby is St. Miguel market. Here traders sell fruit and fish, which is brought from the coast daily. Another popular market is the Rastro. You can buy almost anything in and around Plaza Mayor.

▽ **A sidewalk café** People like to eat and drink in the open air, while other Madrileños and visitors stroll by.

◁ **An artist paints outside the Prado Museum** The statue is of the famous Spanish painter Diego Velázquez.

▽ **Crowds in the Rastro** Street markets on Sunday mornings are full of people looking for a bargain and families enjoying a day out.

LAND OF CASTLES

In the Middle Ages Spain was made up of several kingdoms. Christian kings fought the Moors, an Arab people from Northern Africa, for control of Spain. Warring rulers built huge stone castles to defend their lands. Spain has more castles than any other country in Europe. Most of these castles are in the region of Castile, which was the strongest Christian kingdom. Its queen, Isabella I, married King Ferdinand of Aragón in 1469. Together they united Spain.

From Madrid, you can travel to the region of Castile and Leon by train or bus. Visit the ancient city of Ávila. Here you step back in time as you enter the walled city with its massive gates and round towers. Many Christian pilgrims come here because the city was the birthplace of St. Teresa de Jesús in 1515. Other towns in this region are Segovia and the university city of Salamanca. Segovia is famous for its castle, or *Alcázar*, a marvel of spires and towers. The Alcázar was almost destroyed by fire in the 1800s, but it was carefully restored. Segovia's other marvel is its Roman aqueduct. The huge stone blocks of this water-carrying bridge are fitted together without mortar. The 2,000-year-old aqueduct used to carry water to the town.

South of Madrid is Toledo in the region of Castile La Mancha. Toledo was famous in the Middle Ages for making fine steel swords. The town railroad station is modern, but is built in Moorish style to look like many of the old buildings in southern Spain. Toledo was the hometown of the famous painter El Greco. He was born in Crete but came to live in Toledo in 1577.

▷ **A view across Toledo** Christians, Jews, and Moors lived together in this city in the Middle Ages. Toledo was the capital of Spain for hundreds of years, before Madrid was made capital in the 1500s.

◁ **A local hero** This statue honors Juan Bravo, who led the people of Segovia in a revolt in the 1500s. It stands in the Plaza de San Martín.

▽ **Sixteenth-century homes in Segovia** In some of these houses lived glass workers who produced the windows and mirrors of Spanish royal palaces.

THE HEART OF SPAIN

About an hour's train ride from Madrid is the Escorial Monastery. This fabulous castle, built for King Philip II, was finished in 1584. It was built to be a palace, a library, and a monastery — a place where the king could escape the life of the court in Madrid. All but two of the kings of Spain after Charles V (Philip's father) are buried here. The library has a huge collection of precious books. Many of them are hundreds of years old. In other parts of the building you can see paintings by famous European artists, tapestries, and marvelous wooden furniture.

Central Spain is the high plateau called the Meseta. Winds sweep across the plains from the mountains. There are few large cities in this part of Spain. Most people are farmers. Many herd merino sheep. Others tend cork trees and olive groves.

People in this part of Spain love horses and horsemanship. Life on the Meseta is tough and the region bred tough soldiers. One was Hernán Cortés, the conqueror of Mexico, who came from Medellín. Another was Francisco Pizarro, the conqueror of Peru, who came from Trujillo.

▷ **The village of Albarracín in the region of Aragón** Walls, castle, and houses from the Middle Ages have been carefully preserved.

Spain was once part of the Roman Empire. The Roman amphitheater at Mérida holds 14,000 spectators. It is still used today. Nearby is a Roman track for horse racing.

Many Portuguese tourists visit Badajoz, which is less than 4 miles (6 kilometers) from the border. Badajoz has seen many battles, most recently in the Spanish Civil War. Burgos, in the north of Spain, is the site of earlier battles. Burgos is also the birthplace of Spain's national hero, Rodrigo Díaz de Vivar, known as El Cid. His fight against the Moors is part of Spanish legend.

◁ **Roman amphitheater at Mérida** This 2,000-year-old arena is still the site of a yearly theater festival sponsored by the city of Mérida.

▷ **Olive trees** Olives are among the most important of Spain's crops. Olives may be crushed to make oil or harvested whole for a variety of uses. The trees need a hot, dry climate. They can live for hundreds of years.

FISHERMEN AND MOUNTAINS

North of the Meseta rise the mountains of the region of Galicia – the Cantabrian Cordillera and the Pyrenees. The Pyrenees form the border with France. Northern Spain has a long coastline on the Bay of Biscay, so the sea plays an important part in people's lives here. Spain's fishing fleet is large and modern. Fish are caught far out in the Atlantic Ocean. Spanish people enjoy fresh seafood, including squid, octopus, lobster, and clams. Along the coast are historic ports. La Coruña, with its Roman lighthouse, is one of them. Another old port is Vigo. Here treasure hunters believe a sunken Spanish gold fleet lies on the seabed.

The Galicians are Celts, like the people of Ireland and Scotland. They have their own language and love poetry and music. They also love their green mountains. Galicia gets more rain than any other region of Spain.

The pride of Galicia is Santiago de Compostela. For Christian pilgrims Santiago de Compostela is one of the most interesting places in Europe. Spanish soldiers of old said that they were helped in battle by a vision of St. James, the patron saint of Spain. His tomb lies here in a cathedral that dates from the 1200s.

Cave paintings 25,000 to 30,000 years old were found near Altamira in Cantabria in 1879. These rare examples of prehistoric European art are preserved in caves. Experts come from all over the world to study the bison, horses, and other animals drawn on the rock walls of the Altamira caves.

Like many cities of Spain, Pamplona in the province of Navarre has a center that was built in the Middle Ages. Its people work hard all year. Then in July there is a week-long fiesta. The most famous event is the "running of the bulls." People dash through the streets, running toward the bullring ahead of wild bulls. Many tourists come to see or take part in this famous event.

▽ St. James's Day at Santiago de Compostela Giant models of Christians and Moors are paraded through the streets.

△ Walking through La Coruña Visitors find much to see in Spain's old towns. Buildings of the Middle Ages often stand close to modern offices and stores.

◁ Fishing boats in harbor Spain has a large fishing fleet that includes many big, modern boats. At the front of this picture you can see traps for catching lobsters.

17

BASQUE COUNTRY

The Basques are a people who live on both sides of the Pyrenees Mountains. About 2,500,000 Basques live in Spain and about 500,000 in France. They have their own language, which is unlike either Spanish or French. "Basque" is a French name for the people. They call themselves "Euskaldunak" or "Euskotarak." Basque town names and road signs do not look like the Spanish ones. But most Basques speak Spanish. Spain's Basques have their own region where they govern themselves, but some want complete freedom from Spanish rule.

At the town of Guernica, Basques have met for hundreds of years beside an oak tree to elect their leaders. In 1936, during the Spanish Civil War, the Basques declared their region a republic. Guernica was bombed by airplanes. The bombing inspired the painter Pablo Picasso to create one of the masterpieces of modern art, which he named after this city. Visitors to the Basque country find both elegant resorts, like San Sebastián, and fishing villages. The main Basque city is Bilbao. It is a shipbuilding and steelmaking city and Spain's biggest port.

◁ **A bakery** Many Spanish people like to shop in small local stores like this one in Barcelona, the biggest city in northern Spain and the capital of Catalonia.

▷ **A valley in the Pyrenees** This mountain range divides Spain from France. Many of its peaks rise to over 10,000 feet (3,000 meters).

▷ **A Basque couple in traditional clothing** The clothes are handmade and often decorated with fine lace.

The Basque people are very religious. Like most Spaniards they are Roman Catholics. On special occasions, such as the August festivals held every year, people dress in traditional white shoes and red sashes and carry walking sticks.

Basques are famous for their skill as sailors, whalers, and fishermen. These proud people have their own national sport, a ball game called *pelota*. A more recent version is called *jai alai*. They also enjoy good food. In the markets you can buy fish, cheese made from sheep's milk, and fresh vegetables.

CATALONIA

In the northeast corner of Spain is the province of Catalonia. The province has a rocky Mediterranean coastline called the *Costa Brava*, or Wild Coast. Most Catalans live along the coast, but some live in the mountains. They live in small villages where the red-roofed houses are clustered together. Some make a living by herding sheep. Farmers grow grain and grapes. On market day, they drive into town for a day out.

In Spain you can buy goods in weekly markets that have been held ever since the Middle Ages. The market at La Bisbal, for example, was first held in 1322. The beaches and towns of the Costa Brava are popular with tourists. Inland, the mountain scenery is enjoyed by hikers, horseback riders, and campers. The mountains also offer skiing. Nuria, one of Spain's oldest winter sports centers, is reached by a cogwheel railroad.

△ **Catalans playing a traditional ball game** The game is a form of skittles, or ninepins, played on open ground. The playing circle is marked in the loose sand.

▷ **Walking along La Rambla** Barcelona's most famous avenue has cafés, restaurants, hotels, flower stalls, markets, along with antique, jewelry, and clothes shops.

Catalonia was an independent state before Spain was united. It once ruled some of the Mediterranean islands and parts of Greece. In the early 1900s many of Spain's first large factories were built in Catalonia. The people here speak Catalán, a language more like the French of southern France than the Spanish you will hear in Madrid. The heart of Catalonia is the lively city of Barcelona, the capital of the region.

Barcelona is Spain's second-largest city. In the center is a long boulevard called La Rambla, which leads to a statue of Christopher Columbus. Taking a boat trip around the port is a good way to see the city. Barcelona's landmarks include the Olympic Stadium, built in 1992, and the famous Temple of the Holy Family. This cathedral was designed by Antonio Gaudí, Barcelona's most famous architect. It is not yet finished.

△ **A basketball game** This is being played in the arena that was built for the Olympic Games held in Barcelona in 1992.

MEDITERRANEAN COASTS

Eastern Spain has a long Mediterranean coastline. The *Costa Dorada*, or Golden Coast, and *Costa Blanca*, or White Coast, are both found here. Sunny weather and clear-blue water make this a popular vacation spot. The area is also good for growing crops. The main city, Valencia, is famous for oranges and lemons. In the 1500s and 1600s it was also a prosperous silk and pottery-making city. Here many people speak a form of Catalán, which is different from Spanish. Valencia is Spain's third biggest city. It is a major center for business and industry.

△ **Oranges from Valencia** The warm climate of southern Spain is good for growing citrus and other fruits, such as melons.

◁ **Tourist hotels line the beach at Benidorm** Every year millions of people from other European countries come to Spain for vacations.

▷ **Boats in harbor at Capdepera** This is a town enclosed by walls on the island of Mallorca, the largest of Spain's Balearic Islands.

On the flat plains around Valencia are farms where rice, corn, and vegetables are grown. This is the *huerta*, Spain's best farming region. Farmers have grown crops in fields here for more than 2,000 years. A network of canals carries water to the fields. Without water, very little would grow along this hot, dry coast. The canal system was begun in Roman times. The Moors, who settled here in the Middle Ages, added to it and made it work better. Today the supply and use of water is organized by a council that meets outside.

From either Barcelona or Valencia you can take a ferryboat to the Balearic Islands. Tourists began visiting these Mediterranean islands in the 1800s, but the history of the islands goes back to much earlier times. There are four main islands: Mallorca, Ibiza, Menorca, and Formentera. You will find many prehistoric monuments on Menorca. There are also elegant houses built in the 1700s, when the island was ruled by Britain. Air travel has changed parts of Mallorca. Tourists now flock to high-rise hotel resorts with crowded beaches and night clubs.

THE SOUTH

When people think of Spain, they often think of guitar music, bullfighting, and the lively flamenco dance. You will find all these in the hot, dry south. Here different peoples have come and gone over hundreds of years. They came by sea from Africa and from the eastern Mediterranean. They settled in what is now the region of Andalusia. You can still see old Arab-style buildings. These are reminders of the time when this part of Spain was ruled by the Moors from North Africa. The Moorish kingdoms in Spain were part of the Muslim world.

The city of Granada was Moorish from the 700s until 1492, when the king of Spain took it back. During that time, Granada was a center of Islamic art and learning. The Alhambra at Granada is a palace and fortress built by the Moorish kings. This famous building is admired for the beauty of its decorated courts and halls. Moorish kings enjoyed the cool of its gardens and fountains.

Beside the Guadalquivir River is Córdoba. This city has a mixture of medieval and modern buildings. It too was once Moorish. There is a Christian church inside the walls of its enormous Muslim mosque. A famous Arab doctor named Averroës taught medicine at Córdoba. Maimónides, a Jewish philosopher and doctor, also taught here. He is honored by a monument in the city.

Between Córdoba and the Mediterranean is the town of Guadix. Many of the people here live in caves. They are gypsies, and they love to play the guitar, sing, and dance the flamenco. The guitar was made popular by gypsy music makers. The flamenco is a noisy but very exciting dance.

▷ **Tourists shop for souvenirs** Tourism is an important industry in Spain. Visitors come to see historic cities and to enjoy the beaches on the sunny coastline.

◁ **A village in Granada** The houses are close together. Village streets are often too narrow for cars.

△ **A gypsy child dries corncobs** Many gypsies live in Andalusia. Gypsy influence on the music, traditional costumes, and dance of Spain has been strong.

SEVILLE AND ANDALUSIA

The biggest city in southern Spain is Seville. It has a huge cathedral built in the Gothic style. In the week before Easter there are colorful parades. The *Sevillanos*, or people of Seville, build floats showing scenes from the life and death of Jesus. After Easter comes an April festival of horse-riding, dancing, fireworks, and bullfights.

▽ **A view across Seville** In the foreground is the cathedral. It is the third biggest Gothic church in Europe.

In the 1500s fleets of treasure ships from America brought Inca and Aztec gold and silver to Seville. The city was the main port for Spain's New World Empire. Today, it is the center of Spain's most crowded region. New industries have been started. Roads and railroads have been made much better. The land was once too poor for farming, but irrigation and modern truck-farming methods have made it fertile. Crops of melons and flowers are now grown under glass and plastic. Spain has become a modern industrial nation, but some of its people are still poor, especially in the south.

The region of Andalusia is famous for wines. Sherry was first made in the town of Jerez. From the port of Cádiz, Christopher Columbus sailed to the New World. Today vacationers sun themselves on the beaches of the *Costa del Sol*, or Sun Coast. Others go inland to see birds and other wildlife of Donaña National Park, Spain's finest nature reserve. At the southernmost tip of Spain is the town of Gibraltar, a small British colony. It was named after a Moorish king who came from Africa in A.D. 711 and is most famous for the steep mountain known as the Rock of Gibraltar. From the top of the Rock you can see the coast of Africa.

From Seville's railroad station, express trains speed northward. The trip to Madrid takes less than three hours — a swift and comfortable end to your Spanish journey.

▽ **Arcos de la Frontera** This is a hilltop town above the Guadalete River between Seville and Cádiz.

▽ **The tomb of Columbus in Seville's cathedral** Some experts do not believe that the famous explorer is really buried here.

SPAIN FACTS AND FIGURES

People

Like most Europeans, the Spanish people are a mixture of peoples. Celts, Greeks, Phoenicians, Romans, Germanic peoples, and Moors all settled in Spain in the past. And some Spanish people have ancestors who were born in America or Africa.

Trade and Industry

About four out of every ten of Spain's working people are employed in manufacturing or mining. Industry has grown rapidly since the 1950s. There are steel mills, shipyards, automobile plants, and factories making electrical goods, machinery, textiles, and clothing. Barcelona, Bilbao, and Madrid are the main centers of industry.

Many Spanish people work in service industries, such as public administration, education, and tourism.

Spain has few mineral resources, although it has some iron ore, coal, lead, copper, salt, and other minerals. Most of its ancient forests have been cut down and cleared to make farmland, roads, and towns.

△ **Bullfighters ready to enter the ring**
Bullfighting began in Spain in the 1700s. Bullfighters are known as *matadores*.

Farming

Spain has historically been a backward agricultural country. Its soils are dry and poor. Today fewer people work on farms than ever before. The government has encouraged modern methods, such as irrigation, but many small farmers still use older, more traditional methods.

Important farm crops are olives, barley, wheat, potatoes, oranges, and grapes. Spain is Europe's third biggest wine producer, after Italy and France.

Spanish farmers also grow lettuce and vegetables for sale to other European countries.

Sheep and goats are raised on dry pastures. Cattle are found mainly in northern Spain, where it is cooler and there is more rainfall.

Fishing

Spain has a large and modern fishing fleet. Fishermen catch anchovy, cod, sardine, tuna, squid, and lobster. Mussels, oysters, and other shellfish are also caught. Most of the boats sail from Spain's northern ports.

Food

Spanish people—even those who live far from the sea—eat a lot of fish. Favorite meats include chicken, beef, goat, and lamb.

Many people drink wine with lunch and dinner. People also enjoy *sangria*, a drink made from wine, soda water, fruit juice, and fruit. Coffee and chocolate are other popular drinks.

Lunch, the main meal, is eaten in the middle of the day. Most people eat snacks called *tapas* during the day.

Traditional dishes include:
chorizo: pork sausage highly seasoned with cayenne pepper, pimentos, and garlic
empanadas: a pastry turnover filled with meat
gazpacho: cold soup made from tomatoes, olive oil, and spices
paella: rice flavored with yellow saffron, eaten with chicken, ham, or shrimp and vegetables
queso: cheese, often used as a filling for a *bocadillo*, or long crusty sandwich
tapas: bite-sized snacks of mushrooms, ham, fried eel, crayfish, cheese, and various other ingredients

△ **Flamenco dancers** The colorfully dressed dancers stamp their feet and snap their fingers in time to the music.

Schools

All Spanish children must go to school from the age of five to sixteen. Children spend their first eight years of schooling in primary schools. Most go on to secondary school for three years, from age fourteen to sixteen.

Secondary school students must pass an extra year's course before they can enter a university.

Education in state-run schools is free, but some parents send their children to private Roman Catholic or nonreligious schools.

The Media

Spanish radio and television are run by government-controlled agencies. There are two nationwide TV channels and also numerous local stations. Spanish viewers can also watch satellite channels.

Spain has about 100 daily newspapers. The biggest are *El Pais*, published in Madrid, and *La Vanguarda*, published in Barcelona. Others include *ABC*, *Ya*, and *El Mundo*. Magazines and weekly newspapers are also popular.

Art, Literature, Drama

Spain has produced many great painters. They include El Greco, Diego Velázquez, Francisco de Goya, Joan Miró, Salvador Dalí, and Pablo Picasso — thought by many to be the greatest artist of the 1900s.

Spanish literature began with *The Life of the Cid*, an epic poem written about 1140. The most famous book in Spanish is *Don Quixote*, written by Miguel de Cervantes in 1605. It describes the travels and adventures of a chivalrous but foolish knight and his faithful servant.

The 1600s were a time of great drama, with the verse plays of Lope de Vega and Pedro Calderon de la Barca. Modern Spanish writers include the poet Federico García Lorca.

Spanish music is strongly influenced by folk dance and song. The guitar is the best-known instrument in Spanish music. But other musicians, like Pablo Casals, the famous cello player, have also achieved fame. Spanish culture has developed new forms of art and music among the Spanish-speaking peoples of Mexico and Central and South America.

SPAIN FACTS AND FIGURES

Religion

About 99 percent of Spanish people are Roman Catholics. Until 1978 Roman Catholicism was the official religion in Spain, and only Catholic marriages were legal. Today people of all religions have the same rights in law, and the Church has less power but is still a strong force.

Festivals and Holidays

Church holidays are major national events. Holy Week, the week before Easter, is especially important. There are also local festivities in honor of patron (guardian) saints.

Here are some special holidays:

January 1 **New Year's Day** People eat twelve grapes on New Year's Eve for good luck.

Holy Week, or *Semana Santa* (date varies) People parade the streets with decorated floats.

Easter Celebrates Christ's resurrection. Good Friday is a national religious holiday.

May **St. Isidro** A month of bullfights in Madrid

July **San Fermín** The festival in Pamplona, where people and bulls run in the streets

△ **The Alcázar in Seville** This palace and castle was built in the 1300s of geometric shapes and patterns in the Moorish style.

July 25 **St. James's Day** Celebrates Spain's patron saint

October 12 **Columbus Day** Celebrates the landing of Columbus in the New World (Although Italian, he sailed under the Spanish flag.)

November 1 **All Saints' Day** honors saints of the Catholic Church, followed by **All Souls' Day**, for remembering the dead.

December 25 **Christmas Day** Traditionally a religious holiday, Christmas has now become more commercial as in other countries.

Plants

Much of Spain was once forested, but large areas of ancient woodland have been cleared by farmers and grazing animals. There are grasslands and marshes, mountain meadows, forests, and high plateaus where plants are scarce. In the driest areas, desert-type plants grow.

Animals

Spain has some of the last truly wild areas left in Europe. Here you may see the rare imperial eagle, bearded vulture, lynx, wild boar, and even a brown bear. The ibex is a nimble mountain goat. Storks nest on housetops, and flamingos feed along the mouths of rivers.

Sports

Bullfighting is Spain's national spectacle. Most cities have a bullring. Fighting bulls are bred on special ranches. The most famous matador of all time, Manuel Benítez, was called "El Cordobés," the man from Cordoba.

The biggest sport in Spain is soccer. Other popular sports are pelota (a fast ball game played on a court), tennis, and basketball.

HISTORY

There have been people living in Spain for at least 100,000 years. About 5,000 years ago the early Iberians, a race of people from southern Europe and northern Africa, settled in Spain and built the first towns. Other peoples from the Mediterranean region, including Phoenicians, started colonies in Spain. Celts moved in from northern Europe.

In the 400s B.C. the North African city of Carthage conquered much of Spain. Then Carthage was defeated by the Romans, who made Spain part of their empire. In Spanish, Spain is España, which comes from the Roman name Hispania.

In the 400s A.D. people called the Visigoths took over Spain, which had become Christian. In the 700s Moors arrived from North Africa. They ruled southern Spain until 1492 when the Christians took it back. The powerful kingdoms of Castile and Aragón joined, uniting most of Spain under one ruler.

In the 1500s Spain ruled the Netherlands, the Philippines, and a rich empire in the Americas.

Then Spanish power declined. During the Napoleonic Wars of the 1800s, Spain was invaded by France. Its South American colonies won their freedom from Spanish rule.

Spain became a republic in 1931. After a civil war (1936-1939), General Franco ruled as a dictator from 1939 until his death in 1975. Spain then became a democratic monarchy under King Juan Carlos I and joined the European Community in 1986. The country is now enjoying a period of stability.

LANGUAGE

Spanish is spoken by people throughout Spain, but there are regional variations and different ways of pronouncing words. The official language is Castilian Spanish — the language of Castile. Some people, such as the Basques and Catalans, speak languages other than Spanish. The Basque language is unlike any other European language. Catalán is more like the French of southern France than Spanish. People in the region of Galicia speak gallego, a language that is more like Portuguese.

Useful words and phrases

English	Spanish
One	*uno*
Two	*dos*
Three	*tres*
Four	*cuatro*
Five	*cinco*
Six	*seis*
Seven	*siete*
Eight	*ocho*
Nine	*nueve*
Ten	*diez*
Sunday	*domingo*
Monday	*lunes*
Tuesday	*martes*
Wednesday	*miércoles*

Useful words and phrases

English	Spanish
Thursday	*jueves*
Friday	*viernes*
Saturday	*sábado*
Good morning	*Buenos días*
Good afternoon	*Buenas tardes*
Good evening	*Buenas noches*
Hello	*Hola*
Good-bye	*Adiós*
Please	*Por favor*
Thank you	*Gracias*
Yes/No	*Sí/No*
boy, girl	*chico, chica*
cat, dog	*gato, perro*
How are you?	*¿Cómo está?*

INDEX

Acknowledgments
Book created for Highlights for Children, Inc. by Bender Richardson White.
Editors: Peter MacDonald and Lionel Bender
Designer: Malcolm Smythe
Art Editor: Ben White
Editorial Assistant: Madeleine Samuel
Picture Researcher: Annabel Ossel
Production: Kim Richardson

Maps produced by Oxford Cartographers, England.
Banknotes from Thomas Cook Currency Services.
Stamps from Stanley Gibbons.

Editorial Consultant: Andrew Gutelle
Guide to Spain is approved by the Spanish National Tourist Office, London
Spain Consultant: Araceli Roque Lago, Geographer, Madrid, Spain
Managing Editor, Highlights New Products: Margie Hayes Richmond

Picture credits
DAS = David Simson/DAS Photographs. EU = Eye Ubiquitous, STOL = Spanish Tourist Office, London, Z = Zefa. t = top, b = bottom, l = left, r = right.
Cover: Z/Everts. 6: DAS. 7t: EU/David Cumming. 7b: EU/Peter Buddle. 8, 8-9, 9: EU/David Cumming. 10, 11l, 11r: EU/David Cumming. 12-13, 13t, 13b: STOL. 14: STOL. 15t: EU/David Cumming. 15b: EU/Mike Feeney. 16-17, b: EU/David Cumming. 17tr: STOL. 18: EU/David Cumming. 19t: EU/Peter Thompson. 19b: EU/David Cumming. 20l: EU/Larry Bray. 20-21: EU/David Cumming. 21: STOL. 22bl: DAS. 22tr: EU/John Hulme. 23: STOL. 24-25: STOL. 25t: EU/Mike Southern. 25b: EU/Brian Harding. 26: STOL. 27: EU/Peter Thompson. 27(inset): STOL. 28: EU/Antonio Tornero. 29: STOL. 30: EU/Mike Southern. *Illustration on page 1* by Tom Powers.